December 1978

THE SEA ANCHOR

by the same author

THE FOURSOME
ALPHA BETA

# THE SEA ANCHOR

E. A. Whitehead

Faber & Faber
London

First published in 1975
by Faber and Faber Limited
3 Queen Square London WC1
Printed in Great Britain by
Whitstable Litho, Straker Brothers Ltd

ISBN 0 571 10640 4

THE SEA ANCHOR was first performed at The Theatre Upstairs at the Royal Court in July 1974. The cast was as follows:

| | |
|---|---|
| LES | Peter Armitage |
| ANDY | David Daker |
| SYLVIA | Alison Steadman |
| JEAN | Marjorie Yates |

Directed by Jonathan Hales
Designed by Sue Plummer
Lighting by John Tindale

## CHARACTERS

|  |  |
|---|---|
| ANDY | thirties |
| LES | twenties |
| JEAN | twenties |
| SYLVIA | teens |

The action takes place during a day and the following morning in a jetty in Dublin Bay.

Across the stage runs a promenade with a vividly painted frontage of hotels, boarding houses and souvenir shops. Along the sea edge of the promenade runs a railing to which lifebelts are strapped.
From the centre of the promenade a huge ramp thrusts forward and down into the auditorium. The ramp is made of timber and is supported by rusty iron piers. It is ancient and scarred by years of wear and exposure.

ACT ONE

Scene: Afternoon, bright sunshine. ANDY sits on
the ramp and scans the sea through binoculars. LES
walks along the promenade, stops at the top, scans
the sea, takes a bottle from his pocket and drinks.
Both men wear shirts and jeans; ANDY wears an
anorak and LES the jacket of an old suit. LES carries
a newspaper.


LES: No sign yet?

ANDY: Eh?

LES: No sign of him yet?

ANDY: No.

LES: Fucking hero.

    (LES spits in the water. Comes down the ramp)

ANDY: There's the ferry . . . going back to Liverpool.

LES: It's the Liverpool ferry.

ANDY: (waves) All the best! Good luck!

LES: They'll need it.

ANDY: Tomorrow we'll be on it.

LES: Never mind . . . we've got all day.

ANDY: (leers) And all night, dear . . .

LES: I'll drink to that.

    (LES drinks)

ANDY: I'll join you.

(ANDY takes a long drink. LES watches)

LES: You wanna go easy with that.

(LES squats by ANDY, opens the paper)

There's a big gang of reporters waiting for him at
the hotel. Look at this . . . (reads) "THE SOLO
SAILOR. Nick Anderson, thirty one year old father
of four, sets off on solo sail from Liverpool to Dublin
in a ten foot dinghy. Nick told our reporter that the
voyage was his personal response to the challenge of
the New Elizabethan Age."

(LES hoots)

ANDY: So he got his picture in the paper.

LES: Gloryhound. (pause)

(LES looks through the binoculars)

He's late isn't he?

ANDY: He said about eighteen hours . . .

LES: I thought by now we'd be doing the town.

ANDY: Yeah.

(ANDY takes another drink)

LES: By the time he arrives you're gonna be legless.

ANDY: I'm legless now.

LES: Yeah . . . you had a load on the ferry.

ANDY: It's a tradition. Every year, Nick and me . . .
we get pissed on the ferry coming over, pissed in
Dublin, and pissed on the ferry going back.

LES: And then have a drink in Liverpool.

ANDY: To round off the weekend.

LES: Baffles me why we bothered to bring the girls.

ANDY: I warned you.

LES: What?

ANDY: I told you not to bring Sylvie.

LES: I'd never have heard the last of it.

ANDY: Why?

10

LES: Once Nick invited Jean I had to invite Sylvia.

ANDY: The two of you . . . you're too soft with women. What's the point of bringing your mistress on a dirty weekend? It's worse than bringing your wife. (Silence)

LES: Have you got anything lined up?

ANDY: A beauty.

LES: Who?

ANDY: Fat Annie.

LES: She sounds a beauty.

ANDY: She's shaped like a tent. Lovely. She could sleep six of us. You should have seen her last year with Nick and me. She was insatiable.

LES: Both of you?

ANDY: What a woman. (pause) Nick's the only man I know who can down six pints and come six times in the one night. But Annie . . .

LES: Wish I'd been there.

ANDY: I'll introduce you tonight.

LES: No point -

ANDY: You'll like her.

LES: I'm stuck with Sylvia.

ANDY: Pity.
    (Silence)

LES: It is a pity.

ANDY: You could have had a go at Annie.

LES: Very kind.

ANDY: (genteel) Oh, don't mention it.

LES: I meant kind of her. (pause) Pity, that. I just fancy a bit of strange, too.

ANDY: I had a bit of strange last night.

LES: Did you?

ANDY: Yeah, I fucked the wife. (pause) Whenever I'm

off on a dirty weekend I make sure I fuck the wife
before I go, and she shuts up.

LES: I fuck mine when I get back.

ANDY: You should never neglect your marital obligations.

LES: No.

ANDY: After all a wife is a human being.

LES: Yes.

ANDY: She needs a fuck as much as we do.

LES: That's true.

ANDY: What else is there? A feed, a fuck, a good kip . . .

LES: (arch) Have you ever been in love?

ANDY: In love? Once . . . when I was young and green.
Never again.

LES: Why not?

ANDY: It interfered with the fucking. All this sex talk is
making me thirsty.

LES: Let's go and grab a pint.

ANDY: No . . . we better stay here. He's due now.

LES: He's overdue.

ANDY: Yeah . . .

LES: We're not gonna stay here, are we? All day?

ANDY: Let's hang on for a bit longer.

LES: Hey, Andy . . .

ANDY: Yes, Lesley?

LES: Have you got any Durex?

ANDY: Never use them. I prefer it in the raw.

LES: Catch a dose.

ANDY: I've fucked over 300 women, never caught a dose.
Had a spot of NSU once.

LES: NSU?

ANDY: Pissed hot needles for a week. But never had a
dose.

LES: I wouldn't risk it without a contraceptive.

12

ANDY: I never use them. It's like picking your nose with
your gloves on.

LES: You must leave a trail of bastards behind you.

ANDY: I never stay around to find out.

(Pause)

LES: I wonder if I can get any here?

ANDY: (mock shock) They wouldn't allow such filth in
Ireland! You'll just have to pull out. What's Sylvia
like on the job?

LES: Avid.

ANDY: Oh . . . avid.

LES: When we're on the job she snorts and trumps.

ANDY: The dirty bitch! Hey . . . would she make a
foursome up with Annie?

LES: (looks up the ramp) Ask her.

(JEAN and SYLVIA come down the ramp)

ANDY: Hey, Sylvie . . .

SYLVIA: What?

ANDY: Will you do me a favour?

SYLVIA: What is it?

ANDY: (leers) Nothing, really . . .

SYLVIA: (giggles) Oh, anything for you, Andy.

ANDY: (seizes her) Really?

SYLVIA: Sod off!

ANDY: (nuzzling) Flesh!

SYLVIA: Les . . . help!

ANDY: In five minutes you could make me a happy man.

SYLVIA: Leggo, you're pinching.

ANDY: Are you still wearing that pink corset? I've told
you it's too tight.

SYLVIA: What's the favour?

ANDY: I want you and Les to join me and my lady friend
tonight.

13

SYLVIA: What? For a drink?

ANDY: And for some fun and games . . .

SYLVIA: You can sod off.

ANDY: There . . . what did I say? When a woman's in
love she loses all sense of adventure.

SYLVIA: I'm quite satisfied with Les.

ANDY: But is he satisfied with you?

SYLVIA: I think so.

ANDY: Note of hesitation there.

JEAN: No news yet?

(Pause)

ANDY: No.

JEAN: He's very late, isn't he?

ANDY: You getting impatient?

JEAN: No, but -

LES: Maybe we oughta go and check with the coastguard.

ANDY: Could do . . .

SYLVIA: The hotel bar was packed with reporters.

LES: Did you get a free drink?

SYLVIA: We got two actually. They were very hospitable,
weren't they, Jean?

ANDY: It's an Irish tradition.

LES: Would they be as hospitable to Andy and me?

JEAN: They were just after a story.

ANDY: Which we shall give them! A story of heroism . . .

LES: You can tell he's had a few.

ANDY: You wouldn't understand it.

LES: What?

ANDY: The challenge of the ocean.

LES: It's not an ocean, it's a sea.

ANDY: It's an alien element.

LES: What?

ANDY: It's alien. Makes you feel puny . . . yet big.

14

(LES smiles at the girls and chuckles)

Would you have the guts to tackle that crossing?

LES: No chance.

ANDY: Then you can't talk. (pause) Thank God there are some real men left.

LES: Huh!

ANDY: It's our tradition . . . the English heritage . . . the island race . . .

LES: The armchair Vikings.

ANDY: It's in our blood. Listen, in the last century an Englishman sailed to the Baltic in a converted life-boat. Now thousands of people . . . Look, when I was a kid you never even saw a car in our street in Liverpool. Now you see not just cars but boats as well . . . and at the weekends they'll all off to the Lake District, or the Welsh coast . . . thousands of them, messing about in boats.

LES: It's an excuse for escaping from the wife and kids.

ANDY: You know Nick and me were planning to buy one?

SYLVIA: (impressed) Buy a boat?

ANDY: We've been paying out a fortune in hire charges so we thought we'd buy one between us. Have some fun then . . .

SYLVIA: Great!

LES: What kind of boat?

ANDY: We'd like an ocean racer for nine grand but we'll probably get a second hand dinghy for twenty quid.

LES: Roll on.

ANDY: (leering) Very handy for the weekend.

LES: (sings) "On the good ship Venus
My God you should have seen us . . . "

ANDY: Nice and compact.

LES: (sings) "Wanking on the planking . . . "

15

SYLVIA: Oh Les!

LES: What?

SYLVIA: I think it sounds marvellous.

ANDY: Yes, we could have some nice weekends down in Holyhead.

SYLVIA: Could I come?

ANDY: There's a bench reserved for you.

LES: What's wrong with the back of the car?

SYLVIA: That's all I ever get from him.

LES: Haven't heard you complain.

SYLVIA: I hate making love in the back of a car.

LES: Try the front if you like.

SYLVIA: Is that all you want me for?

LES: What?

SYLVIA: You know what.

LES: What?

SYLVIA: Sex.

LES: I thought that was what you wanted me for?

SYLVIA: I think you _are_ sex-obsessed.

LES: If you'd let me know how you felt I would've made alternative arrangements.

(Silence. ANDY stands, scans the sea)

ANDY: No . . . you can't beat it. I remember one Saturday morning, cruising off Holyhead, a few weeks back. I got up very early, put the breakfast on . . . Nick was still snoring. I came out and had my first piss of the day. I remember standing there . . . there wasn't a soul in sight . . . just a tiny twist of smoke on the horizon . . . and all I could hear was the waves sucking the hull . . . fibreglass hull . . . the cry of a seabird . . . and the bacon sizzling on the old Primus! I stood there, stretched out my arms, filled the old lungs with

16

ozone, and I thought: "This is the life."

LES: Here we go again.

ANDY: The sea is different from the land.

LES: Yes, it's the water.

ANDY: Don't you feel it?

LES: What?

ANDY: (<u>arch</u>) The lure of the deep.

LES: The lure of my arse.

ANDY: Don't you feel the romance of sailing?

SYLVIA: He hasn't an ounce of romance in him.

ANDY: Don't you?

LES: You know what cured me of the romance of sailing?

ANDY: What?

LES: Three years in the Merchant Marine.

ANDY: That's not sailing. That's like working in a
        floating factory. Might just as well be on land. Now
        in a pocket cruiser or a dinghy -

SYLVIA: Hey, could we go for a sail?

LES: We're going for a sail.

SYLVIA: When?

LES: Tomorrow, on the ferry.

SYLVIA: I mean in a boat. A little boat. Could we?

LES: You go.

SYLVIA: Will you?

LES: No.

SYLVIA: Why not?

LES: I don't want to.

SYLVIA: Oh, please Les . . . I'd love to go for a sail.

LES: I don't like sailing.

SYLVIA: Why not?

LES: The sea can drown you.

ANDY: Where's your spirit of adventure, man?

LES: (<u>points between his legs</u>) Here.

17

(SYLVIA slaps LES lightly)

SYLVIA: Cheeky bugger! Nick didn't have much
   experience of sailing, but look at him, sailing the
   Irish Sea . . .

LES: That proves he's a real man.

SYLVIA: Yes.

LES: (tough guy tones) Well, either you've got it or you
   haven't, I guess. (pause) I tell you one thing. I'd
   rather be sitting here than sitting out there. (laughs)
   Huh . . .

ANDY: Whatever you say about Nick, he's a man. He
   does exactly what he wants to do. He's a real man.
   (pause) I never really thought he'd do it.

SYLVIA: What made him do it?

ANDY: It was just a . . . a sudden decision. We were
   talking about our weekend here . . . you know,
   planning the trip on the ferry . . .

JEAN: Planning the orgy?

ANDY: We never plan our orgies.

JEAN: Don't you?

ANDY: We just create conditions that are conducive to
   them.

JEAN: Huh . . . conducive!

ANDY: Anyway, I happened to mention these students
   that were gonna sail from Blackpool to the Isle of
   Man on a mattress. (laughs) On a mattress! I thought
   they were nuts . . . But Nick was very impressed.
   The next thing I knew he was buying sailing magazines
   and talking like an old salt. Spent a fortune on charts
   and almanacs.

(Silence. LES takes a drink from the bottle. Passes
it to SYLVIA, who drinks. She offers it to JEAN,
who refuses. Passes it to ANDY, who drinks)

18

LES: Maybe we ought to organise shifts?

JEAN: Could he have gone in another part of the harbour?

ANDY: No, he'd come in here. Easier to tie up here.

(pause) Anyway . . . if he came in the coastguards would let us know.

JEAN: I think we ought to go and ask them.

ANDY: Ask them what?

JEAN: About Nick.

(Silence)

SYLVIA: Where are we going tonight?

ANDY: Everywhere!

SYLVIA: Are there as many pubs as people say?

ANDY: Oh aye, it's a very civilised city.

SYLVIA: I can't wait . . .

ANDY: We'll go to Mooney's, you'll like that.

SYLVIA: Has it got a juke box?

ANDY: It's full of dockers and coalmen.

SYLVIA: Thanks very much!

ANDY: What's wrong with dockers and coalmen?

SYLVIA: Is there anywhere we can have a dance?

ANDY: (mock shock) Dance?

SYLVIA: I'd enjoy a dance. Wouldn't you, Jean?

ANDY: Sylvia darling . . . we're not going out to enjoy ourselves, we're going out boozing. If you want entertainment we'll go to Searson's.

SYLVIA: Do they have a show?

ANDY: Yes . . . you can always count on a good punch-up.

SYLVIA: Huh . . .

(SYLVIA grimaces. Takes a swig from the bottle and passes it to LES. He drinks then tosses the bottle into the water)

LES: That's killed that.

ANDY: Nick'll pass it on the way in.

LES: I shoulda stuck a message in to say we'd be in the alehouse.

ANDY: He's missed the tide.

LES: Yeah . . .

(SYLVIA scans the sea through the binoculars)

SYLVIA: It's nice and clear.

(She offers the binoculars to JEAN)

JEAN: No . . . once I start looking I'll never stop.

(SYLVIA looks up and follows the flight of a bird)

SYLVIA: Oh, look at this bird.

ANDY: Beautiful.

SYLVIA: Wish I could fly.

LES: You lot should have been birds and fishes.

(Silence)

ANDY: It's nearly half four.

LES: Yeah . . .

ANDY: You think we should go and have a talk to the coastguards?

LES: Might as well.

ANDY: See what they say . . .

LES: Be here all day otherwise. And all night.

(ANDY and LES stand)

JEAN: I'll come with you.

ANDY: No, you stay here.

JEAN: I wanna hear what they say.

ANDY: He'll probably come sailing in soon as we go.

JEAN: Oh . . . all right. Will you come straight back?

ANDY: Promise. We'll only be a few minutes.

SYLVIA: No diversions, now.

LES: What?

SYLVIA: If you're going to the alehouse I'm coming with you.

LES: We'd never dream of going to the pub without you.

SYLVIA: Hmmm.

ANDY: And we'll bring a bottle back with us.

JEAN: Huh!

ANDY: Relax . . . talk about us while we're gone.

    (ANDY and LES go off. SYLVIA sits)

SYLVIA: (jumps) Jesus! That's hot . . . feels as if it's
    gonna burst into flame. (wriggles) Your knickers
    stick to your arse.

    (Pause. SYLVIA examines the woodwork, brushes
    it, examines her dress, brushes that)

    Do you think this dress looks all right?

JEAN: Very sexy.

SYLVIA: (giggles) That's what Les said.

JEAN: Does he like it?

SYLVIA: Oh, he can't stand it.

JEAN: Why?

SYLVIA: He'd have me wearing a boiler suit all the time.

JEAN: Is he very jealous?

SYLVIA: He's mad. Mind you . . . I'm jealous myself.

JEAN: Are you?

SYLVIA: Aren't you?

JEAN: I can be.

SYLVIA: You're bound to be jealous if you're really in
    love. (pause) Do you feel jealous of Nick's wife?

JEAN: No.

SYLVIA: Don't you?

JEAN: You wanna see her.

SYLVIA: What's she like?

JEAN: Fat.

SYLVIA: Is she? Mind you . . . she's had four kids,
    hasn't she?

JEAN: She's still fat.

SYLVIA: Yeah. I'd hate to be fat. (pause) Mind you, I'd
    like to have kids, wouldn't you?

JEAN: No thanks!

SYLVIA: Wouldn't you?

JEAN: No.

SYLVIA: I don't mean I want them now . . . but, you
    know, later.

JEAN: Later?

SYLVIA: When I'm older. I think kids give you something
    to live for when you're older.

JEAN: I've got something to live for already.

SYLVIA: What?

JEAN: Me.

    (SYLVIA giggles. Silence)

SYLVIA: Would your husband like kids?

JEAN: Oh, he would . . .

SYLVIA: Would he?

JEAN: Yes, to tie me down.

SYLVIA: What did you tell him about the weekend?

JEAN: Said I was gonna spend it with my mate in
    Nottingham.

SYLVIA: Does he mind?

JEAN: He doesn't have any choice.

SYLVIA: Does he believe you?

JEAN: He'd swallow anything.

SYLVIA: And have you really got a mate in Nottingham?

JEAN: Yes. She wouldn't let me down. She couldn't
    afford to.

SYLVIA: Eh?

JEAN: She uses me as an excuse whenever she wants a
    dirty weekend.

SYLVIA: That's awful, that . . .

JEAN: What?

22

SYLVIA: The way people say "dirty weekend." You go
away with someone you love and they call it a "dirty
weekend"! Huh . . . it sounds like me mother.
(pause) I could do with an arrangement like yours . . .
with your mate.

JEAN: I don't know . . . it's too easy.

SYLVIA: What?

JEAN: Sometimes I wish I could just tell my husband
the truth.

SYLVIA: Tell him the truth!

JEAN: Yes

SYLVIA: Why?

JEAN: It'd be simpler.

SYLVIA: What would he do?

JEAN: I don't know. Collapse, I suppose.

SYLVIA: Would he?

JEAN: Yeah.

(Both women laugh)

SYLVIA: Does he have anyone else?

JEAN: How do you mean?

SYLVIA: I mean . . . does he have any affairs?

JEAN: I wish he would.

SYLVIA: Do you? Really?

JEAN: Yes, I do. But he lives for me.

SYLVIA: (smiles) Does he?

JEAN: Stupid bastard.

SYLVIA: Oh, Jean!

JEAN: He's like a big baby. If I say "Boo" to him he goes
off into a mood . . . won't eat, can't sleep and has
a headache all week. See what you're missing?

SYLVIA: Missing?

JEAN: You're free.

SYLVIA: Who . . . me?

23

JEAN: Yes . . . you can do what you like.

SYLVIA: You haven't met my mother.

JEAN: What's she like?

SYLVIA: Oh, she's a terror. She's still living in the
nineteenth century. You know . . .

JEAN: Yes.

SYLVIA: She hasn't got a clue about what goes on in the
world.

JEAN: Does she know about Les?

SYLVIA: You must be joking! A married man? She'd
throw me out.

JEAN: Would she?

SYLVIA: I had to spin a yarn to get away for the weekend.

JEAN: What did you say?

SYLVIA: Said I was gonna see an old mate of mine in
London.

JEAN: Who's the mate?

SYLVIA: That's the trouble.

JEAN: What?

SYLVIA: I haven't got one.

(They laugh)

If only you could be honest about it . . .

JEAN: When you think of all the effort we put into planning
and plotting . . .

SYLVIA: Yeah . . .

JEAN: All of us . . . the men and all . . .

SYLVIA: I know . . .

JEAN: If we put it into a business we'd all be millionaires!

SYLVIA: We would and all. (pause) But what else can we
do?

JEAN: Sometimes I feel like just going down to Lime
Street and getting the first train out and just . . .

24

vanishing.

SYLVIA: Sometimes I feel the same.

JEAN: Why don't you get a flat?

SYLVIA: That's what Les says.

JEAN: Why don't you?

SYLVIA: He said once that if I got a flat then he'd leave home and join me.

JEAN: He said that?

SYLVIA: Yes. When he was drunk.

(Silence)

Anyway . . . they all say that, don't they?

JEAN: Who?

SYLVIA: Married men.

JEAN: Nick never said it to me.

SYLVIA: I'm just so uncertain . . .

JEAN: You mean about Les?

SYLVIA: What?

JEAN: You mean about the way you feel for Les?

SYLVIA: Oh no. No . . . I've always been certain about that, ever since we first met.

JEAN: Have you?

SYLVIA: Yes.

(Silence. JEAN studies SYLVIA)

JEAN: What's the problem then?

SYLVIA: It's just . . . making the first move, like.

(pause) Les left home once before, you know.

JEAN: Did he?

SYLVIA: Yes.

JEAN: Did he get a flat?

SYLVIA: He went to live with some girl in Manchester.

JEAN: What happened?

SYLVIA: He said he got sacked from his job and had to go back home. And his wife was hysterical and there were the kids . . . and . . .

JEAN: Yes.

SYLVIA: So . . . I don't know.

JEAN: God, these wives.

(Silence)

SYLVIA: Are you hoping to get together with Nick?

JEAN: I don't know.

SYLVIA: You've been going with him for ages, haven't you?

JEAN: Five years.

SYLVIA: But aren't you miserable, just . . . just . . .

JEAN: "Drifting"?

SYLVIA: Yes.

JEAN: If you can drift along in marriage you can drift along in adultery.

SYLVIA: I hate that word!

JEAN: What?

SYLVIA: "Adultery".

JEAN: Huh . . . that's the word. (laughs) Anyway, as Nick always says, it's only adultery after sunset.

SYLVIA: What?

JEAN: In the eyes of the law.

SYLVIA: It sounds so ugly.

JEAN: Well, that's the word.

SYLVIA: I mean, you have a serious relationship with Nick. You've known each other five years. Les and me . . . we've only known each other six weeks.

JEAN: That's your strength.

SYLVIA: What?

JEAN: Your strength is that you've only known each other six weeks. My weakness is that we've known each other five years.

(Silence)

26

SYLVIA: But isn't there any hope you'll ever get together?

JEAN: Nick lives in hope.

SYLVIA: Would he leave his family?

JEAN: He hopes they'll get run over or die suddenly in
their sleep.

SYLVIA: Oh . . .

JEAN: I don't know whether I'd want him to leave them.

SYLVIA: Don't you?

JEAN: I don't know how that would work out. (pause)
Things are pretty cushy for me at home. I've got
my husband, and he's . . . all right. He never
interferes and he's always there. Whereas with
Nick . . . huh!

SYLVIA: What -

JEAN: I wouldn't want to take the place of his wife. I
wouldn't put up with it.

SYLVIA: But if you and he were together . . .

JEAN: What?

SYLVIA: Wouldn't that be different?

JEAN: Yes . . . then he'd be trampling over me instead
of her.

SYLVIA: Oh . . .

JEAN: Nick isn't the one-woman type.

SYLVIA: Isn't he?

JEAN: No.
    (Silence)
He's been unfaithful.

SYLVIA: When?

JEAN: When?

SYLVIA: When has he been unfaithful?

JEAN: A few times.

SYLVIA: I mean . . . in the morning, or . . .

JEAN: (laughs) Or after sunset? I don't think the hour of

the day affects me.

(Pause)

SYLVIA: No, no. Oh well . . . it's always the same with a marries man, isn't it?

JEAN: And what about Les?

SYLVIA: What?

JEAN: How do you feel about Les?

SYLVIA: I've never felt about anyone the way I feel about Les.

JEAN: What, never?

SYLVIA: No.

JEAN: Your first love?

SYLVIA: Yes. Don't you believe me?

JEAN: I believe you. And how does Les feel?

SYLVIA: He says I'm the first woman he's ever really loved.

JEAN: Congratulations.

(Silence)

SYLVIA: You don't like him, do you?

JEAN: Who . . . Les?

SYLVIA: Yes.

JEAN: He's not really my type.

SYLVIA: What do you mean?

JEAN: He's too hard.

SYLVIA: Les isn't hard!

JEAN: Isn't he?

SYLVIA: I know he acts hard, but . . . but that is only an act.

JEAN: Is it?

SYLVIA: We all do that, don't we?

(Silence. SYLVIA glances around at the promenade, then more quietly)

I'm dreading telling him I've started.

28

JEAN: You've started?

SYLVIA: Yes. My period.

JEAN: I would've thought he'd have been relieved?

SYLVIA: He'll say I've ruined the weekend. (pause)
Jean . . .

JEAN: What?

SYLVIA: I don't suppose you've got any towels?

JEAN: Towels?

SYLVIA: I didn't expect to start till next week, but I
suppose with all the excitement . . . anyway I was
caught without any sanitary towels. I've had to use
cotton wool.

JEAN: You still use towels, do you?

SYLVIA: Yes.

JEAN: I always use Tampax. I might have one at the
hotel . . .

SYLVIA: I can't use them.

JEAN: (laughs) Oh, Sylvia! Everyone can!

SYLVIA: I've tried. I can't get it in.

JEAN: Why?

SYLVIA: I'm too tight.

JEAN: You're not putting it in properly. Let's see if I've
got any at the hotel, and if I have I'll show you how
to put it in.

SYLVIA: Will you?

JEAN: Yes.

SYLVIA: I hope you have.

JEAN: We must be able to get some anyway. After all,
even the Irish have periods!

(SYLVIA sees the men on the promenade)

SYLVIA: Shhhh.

(Silence. ANDY comes down the ramp, followed by
LES)

ANDY: They've called an alert.

JEAN: An alert?

SYLVIA: Oh God!

ANDY: Don't panic . . .

SYLVIA: I hope he's all right.

ANDY: They would have waited a bit longer but they've
   had a flash from the Met Office. There's some
   dirty weather on the way.

JEAN: What do they do?

ANDY: They alert vessels in the sea area. And they send
   out the helicopters to do a pattern search, and the
   lifeboats . . .

SYLVIA: I hope they find him . . .

ANDY: He's in a busy channel, and it'll be light for a
   while yet.

SYLVIA: Thank God for that.

ANDY: They should spot him pretty quickly.

JEAN: What did they say?

ANDY: What?

JEAN: What did they think could have happened?

ANDY: He might have had a spot of engine trouble . . .
   the outboard might have packed in for some reason.
   Or he might just have gone off course. (pause) They
   contacted the English coastguard.

JEAN: The English?

ANDY: Yes . . . in case he'd gone back.

JEAN: He'd never have gone back.

ANDY: They had no news of him.

   (Silence)

SYLVIA: What'll we do?

LES: Let's all go and have a drink somewhere.

ANDY: We'd better be at the hotel . . . just in case . . .

LES: We could let them know where we're going.

30

ANDY: I've gotta go back to the hotel anyway, to ring his
    wife.

JEAN: Nick's wife?

ANDY: She rang earlier . . . left a message at the hotel.

JEAN: What message?

ANDY: She just asked if Nick would ring her when he came
    in. I better let her know . . .

JEAN: The bitch couldn't wait.
    (JEAN walks up the ramp)

SYLVIA: Jean . . . are you going back to the hotel?
    (JEAN goes off without answering)
    Oh God . . .

LES: What?

SYLVIA: I wonder what's happened to him?

LES: Either he's afloat, in which case he'll turn up
    sooner or later. Or he's not, in which case he won't.

SYLVIA: Don't say that.

LES: Nothing we can do.
    (SYLVIA starts up the ramp. LES takes her arm
    but she shrugs him off)
    Where are you going?

SYLVIA: The hotel.

LES: Let's go and have a drink somewhere.

SYLVIA: I'm going back to the hotel.

LES: What for?

SYLVIA: Jean's gonna get me some Tampax.
    (SYLVIA goes off)

LES: I hope it chokes you.

ANDY: I better go and ring his wife.

LES: What are you gonna say?

ANDY: Make a date for next week. (pause) Jean's a
    right little cow, isn't she?

LES: She's a match for Nick.

31

ANDY: Huh . . . She's worse than his wife. She's been driving Nick nuts lately, you know.

LES: Has she?

ANDY: His wife turns a blind eye to his whoring around but Jean . . . Jesus!

LES: Like having a second wife.

ANDY: Yeah. Well . . . I better go and ring her. (grimaces) Oh, I hate talking to that woman. She'll be hysterical . . .

LES: Then we can go and inspect a few alehouses, eh?

ANDY: What about Jean?

LES: What about her?

ANDY: Hadn't we better stay with her?

LES: She won't thank you for it.
        (ANDY starts up the ramp)
        What about your girl friend?

ANDY: Who?

LES: Annie.

ANDY: (smiles) Oh . . . Fat Annie?

LES: You gonna ring her?

ANDY: I don't know . . .

LES: Tell her about me.

ANDY: Why? You game?

LES: Always game.

ANDY: I don't know . . .

LES: Why don't we go and see her now?

ANDY: I think I better stay with Jean. You coming?
        (ANDY goes off. LES watches him go, then turns and looks seawards)

LES: Bang goes me night in Dublin!
        (LES picks up the newspaper and looks at the picture of Nick in the boat. Tears up the paper and throws it into the sea) BLACKOUT

32

ACT TWO

Scene: Late night. A yellow fog. The ramp dimly
illuminated by the lamps on the promenade. JEAN
sits huddled in a coat and scarf. Distant foghorns.
ANDY comes along the promenade. Peers down the
ramp, then comes down to JEAN.

ANDY: You'll catch your death.
(ANDY sits)
Be a bit more comfortable in the hotel.
(Silence)
I was up at the Coastguards. Hell of a job in this
weather. The fog . . .
(ANDY takes out a bottle, offers it to JEAN, who
ignores it. He drinks)
They're still out there . . . still searching. Hell of
a job. (pause) The reporters have gone home. Les
went into town for a drink with Sylvie. The hotel's
dead.
(ANDY studies JEAN. Silence. Then he hugs her)
Don't worry . . .
JEAN: Huh.
ANDY: If he doesn't make it, you can sleep with me.
JEAN: Thanks.
ANDY: Does he know I'm the other man?

(Silence)

JEAN: What did his wife say?

ANDY: What?

JEAN: You rang her, didn't you?

ANDY: Aye, I rang her.

JEAN: What did she have to say?

ANDY: She asked me to give you her regards and said to remember you're always one of the family.

JEAN: What was her reaction?

ANDY: Hysterical.

JEAN: Huh . . .

ANDY: Whenever I speak to that woman she seems to be in the state of, or on the verge of the state of, hysteria.

JEAN: What did she say?

ANDY: You want to know? (pause) She said Nick was a child who'd been led astray by bad companions.

JEAN: That'd be the day . . .

ANDY: What?

JEAN: Nick led astray . . .

ANDY: And she said that she was sick of him tomcatting around and making a fool of himself with some little slut.

JEAN: Huh! What did you say?

ANDY: (pompous) I agreed.

JEAN: Of course.

ANDY: I agreed with every word she said.

JEAN: You would.

ANDY: My wife was standing next to her.

(Pause)

JEAN: Is she a friend of your wife's?

ANDY: Not exactly a friend -

JEAN: What?

34

ANDY: More of an ally. (laughs) Yes, his missus and
      mine, they're old allies. The two of them are waiting
      up tonight in our house.

JEAN: I bet she's revelling in every minute of it.

ANDY: It's a rare chance.

JEAN: Was that all she said?

ANDY: Apart from a few shrieks and moans. Oh, and
      she said she didn't know what was gonna become of
      her and the kids, because Nick hasn't paid the
      insurance for over six months.

JEAN: That sounds like her.
      (Silence)
      I wonder what he's doing now . . .

ANDY: I bet he's dying for a pint.

JEAN: I bet he's wishing he'd come with us on the ferry.

ANDY: He's probably drifting.

JEAN: Drifting?

ANDY: Yeah . . . he'll know they're looking for him by
      now.
      (Silence)

JEAN: I can't imagine it . . . out there . . .

ANDY: It's not so bad.

JEAN: Isn't it?

ANDY: It's fascinating.

JEAN: In that fog?

ANDY: I remember one time a few weeks back Nick and
      me were caught in a fog. We'd been practising a
      spot of celestial navigation -

JEAN: What?

ANDY: Celestial navigation . . . sailing by the stars. We
      ran into a real pea-souper. Couldn't see a thing.
      And then after a while it lightened and the visibility
      was about fifty yards. The light was yellow and the

35

sea was all black and placid. It was strange . . .
eerie. And then we heard this hissing sound and we
saw this thing like a wave coming at us . . . not
really a wave, though, more like a giant ripple . . .

JEAN: A ripple?

ANDY: Yeah . . . a giant ripple, V-shaped, about five
yards across and seven yards fore and aft . . . and
it came hissing along just by the boat.

JEAN: What was it?

ANDY: We didn't have a clue . . . till it passed by. And
then Nick said: "It's mackerel. It's a shoal of
mackerel!" And they were so close you could have
dipped your hand in and picked a few up.

JEAN: What happened?

ANDY: This great "V" went hissing off into the sea.

JEAN: Wierd.

> (Silence)

What time is it?

ANDY: Near midnight.

> (ANDY offers the bottle to JEAN, who shakes her
> head. ANDY drinks)

Fancy Les going off into town.

JEAN: He would.

> (Silence)

ANDY: I hadn't realised how bad things were between
Nick and his wife.

JEAN: What?

ANDY: She said that he came in about four o'clock in the
morning one night last week -

JEAN: What night?

ANDY: She didn't say. Anyway, she made him something
to eat . . .

JEAN: She waits up for him.

36

ANDY: Yeah . . . anyway, she asked him where he'd
     been and he stuck the breadknife through the coffee
     table. (pause) So . . . she screamed at him and he
     stood up and spat in her face.

JEAN: Oh . . . lately he's been . . . he's been going
     berserk.

ANDY: I know he's been throwing it back.

JEAN: Eh?

ANDY: The booze.

JEAN: Oh yes . . . he drinks all day, and he's never at
     work and he's deep in debt . . . he's in debt up to
     his neck, you know . . . and he worries, and then
     he drinks even more . . .

ANDY: If he didn't drink he might shoot himself.

JEAN: Or he might get some work done.

ANDY: I don't know . . .

JEAN: And he's playing around more than ever. Anything
     in a skirt . . .
     (Silence)

ANDY: His wife asked me to have a talk with him.

JEAN: A talk?

ANDY: Yeah, she said . . . she asked if I'd have a talk
     with him. A fatherly talk. Give him some sensible
     advice, like. Tell him to mend his ways before it's
     too late.

JEAN: She must have a lot of faith in your influence.

ANDY: She has.

JEAN: And in you . . .

ANDY: She knows me as a quiet religious man devoted
     to his family and his dog.

JEAN: Does your wife believe that?

ANDY: She prefers to believe that. Though I don't
     know . . . I am like that . . . by and large.

JEAN: I offered to do something for Nick that his wife
would never do.

ANDY: What?

JEAN: Leave him.

ANDY: Leave him?

JEAN: Yes . . . free him.

ANDY: What did he say?

JEAN: Said he didn't want to be free of me.

ANDY: I don't think he does.

JEAN: He acts like it.

ANDY: Yeah, but . . . (pause) It's tough for his wife,
though, with four kids.

JEAN: Nobody forced her to have them.
(Silence)

ANDY: I think we all worry too much about these things.
You know, we create drama -

JEAN: Do you think I ought to leave him?

ANDY: No. No, he depends on you.

JEAN: I left him for a week a few months back . . . but
he started ringing every day, and meeting me outside
the office, and in the end . . . inevitably . . . we
got back together again. But the only time he pays
me that kind of attention is when I do leave him. It's
no basis for a relationship, is it?

ANDY: (breezy) We're all like that.

JEAN: I'm not.

ANDY: You're a woman.

JEAN: I wouldn't put up with it except that there's just no
other man who's given me what he gives me. And
I've had plenty . . . (pause) I can't imagine living
without Nick. And every so often I could strangle
him.

ANDY: That's natural.

38

(Silence)

You know . . . out there, out at sea . . . it's strange.
You feel as if you're the only thing living and yet all
around, only feet away, are millions of life forms.

JEAN: (shivers) I'd find that very scary.

ANDY: I find it reassuring.

JEAN: Do you?

ANDY: (laughs) Depending on the forms of life.

JEAN: How do you mean?

ANDY: There was one time both of us were terrified. We
saw a fin break surface near the boat, then another,
then another. Fins popping up everywhere. I grabbed
an oar and shouted to Nick: "SHARKS!" I thought we
were gonna be eaten alive.

JEAN: I didn't know there were sharks off England.

ANDY: Oh, sometimes . . . anyway, we stood there
gripping the oars and looking at these black bodies,
big buggers, leaping up and down in the sea. It was
night and the sea was silver and we could see them
flashing up and down. And we could hear them
barking . . . kind of a hoarse barking. And then
Nick said: "Jesus, they're playing!" Sharks don't
play. And we realised they were a school of
porpoises. Yeah, they were porpoises, big soft
buggers, a big gang of them, dancing all round the
boat, playing together.

JEAN: (laughing) Oh . . .

ANDY: We were so relieved we started laughing and
shouting out to them. Our voices were booming in
the fog, all hollow. And they took fright and shot
away through the fog . . . still barking. I'll never
forget them.

JEAN: That's something new to think about.

ANDY: What?

JEAN: Sharks.

ANDY: No . . . no, it's a million-to-one chance. At
     least, at sea, you know who your friends are and
     who your enemies.

JEAN: Why take such risks?

ANDY: Why not?

JEAN: I don't see the point.

ANDY: You can step off the side and get run over any day.

JEAN: Les was right, for once.

ANDY: What?

JEAN: He said you were as crazy as Nick.

ANDY: It was perfectly feasible. It was a perfectly
     feasible exercise. I admire him immensely for
     doing it.

JEAN: You would.

ANDY: You forget . . . men receive knighthoods for
     such . . . feats.

JEAN: (scoffing) Knighthoods . . .

ANDY: Yes.

JEAN: Men receive knighthoods for writing songs
     nowadays.

ANDY: That's different.

JEAN: Is it?

ANDY: Course it is! But when a man does something
     really heroic I think it's only right that it should be
     recognised. And I for one salute him.
     (ANDY takes a swig from the bottle)
     Yes I do!
     (ANDY salutes)
     I salute Nick and all men like him. Because they
     restore my faith in human nature. Because they're
     the real men . . . they do something with their

40

lives while the rest of us sit on our backsides and -

JEAN: Did his wife really say that about me?

ANDY: What?

JEAN: The "little slut" . . .

ANDY: She didn't name any names.

JEAN: Oh . . .

ANDY: No. She might have been talking about somebody else.

JEAN: I see.

(SYLVIA comes along the promenade. ANDY hears her, turns)

ANDY: That you, Sylvie?

JEAN: Yes.

ANDY: Come and join the party.

(SYLVIA steps down the ramp, unsteadily. ANDY helps her down)

Christ . . . I thought you were gonna dive in then. You had a skinful?

SYLVIA: Yeah . . .

ANDY: Where is he then?

SYLVIA: God, I'm freezing.

ANDY: Put this round you.

(ANDY offers his anorak)

SYLVIA: I'm all right.

ANDY: Put it on.

(ANDY helps her into the anorak. They sit)

SYLVIA: What about you?

ANDY: What?

SYLVIA: You'll be cold.

ANDY: I'll cuddle up to you.

(ANDY hugs her)

SYLVIA: (smiles) Sod off.

ANDY: Where is he then?

SYLVIA: Who?

ANDY: Bluebeard.

SYLVIA: Oh, he's in the pub. I left him in the pub.

ANDY: (seizes her) Is there time for a quick one before
    he comes back?

SYLVIA: Lay off.

ANDY: Jean'll keep watch.

SYLVIA: Don't . . .

    (ANDY releases her and she sits slumped)

ANDY: What's the matter?

SYLVIA: I feel sick.

ANDY: You won't throw up on my anorak, will you?

SYLVIA: No . . .

ANDY: Is there anything the matter?

    (Silence)

SYLVIA: No news?

ANDY: No.

    (SYLVIA whimpers)

    Have a drop of this.

SYLVIA: I couldn't.

ANDY: You'll feel better.

SYLVIA: I couldn't take it.

ANDY: It'll warm you up.

SYLVIA: No . . . I've had too much to drink already.

ANDY: (mock moralising) See . . . there you are . . .
    serves you right . . . a young girl like you, out
    drinking with married men . . .

SYLVIA: He wouldn't come outa the pub.

ANDY: What pub?

SYLVIA: A pub in town.

ANDY: (laughs) Did you expect him to?

SYLVIA: I was feeling unwell. (sobs) It was horrible in
    there. All smoky and scruffy and all full of men.

ANDY: Sounds just like home.

SYLVIA: I was feeling dizzy and there was nowhere to sit.
I had to hold onto the bar. And Les . . . Les said I
was making a show of myself in front of the men.
But when I asked him to go he wouldn't, he told me
to . . . "Fuck off." So I hit him.

ANDY: (laughs) You hit Les?

SYLVIA: I slapped him and then I ran out.

JEAN: Good for you.

SYLVIA: All the men were laughing.

(Silence)

All those men in there . . .

ANDY: What?

SYLVIA: They were all standing there with their pints in
their hands looking at me as if they'd never seen a
woman before.

ANDY: Over here they lead sheltered lives.

(Silence)

You're trembling.

SYLVIA: I'll be all right.

ANDY: You'd better go to bed.

SYLVIA: I'm all right.

ANDY: Don't take any notice of Les.

SYLVIA: What?

ANDY: You know what he's like when he's had a few.

SYLVIA: It's too much . . .

ANDY: What?

SYLVIA: I'm browned off with it . . .

ANDY: What you need is a good kip.

SYLVIA: No . . . I'm sick of it . . . I'm sick of all of
it . . .

ANDY: You'll feel better in the morning . . .

SYLVIA: I'm through with it all.

43

ANDY: Come on . . . I'll take you back to the hotel.

(ANDY takes her arm, half rises. SYLVIA doesn't move)

SYLVIA: No . . .

ANDY: Come on.

SYLVIA: I wanna stay here.

ANDY: Why?

SYLVIA: I wanna stay here with you.

ANDY: Come on back. You won't miss anything.

SYLVIA: I'll be all right in a while.

(Silence. ANDY sits back. Drinks. Offers the drink to the women. Neither takes it. After a moment a torch flashes on the promenade. LES comes on and walks to the top of the ramp. Holds the rail and peers down at the others. Flashes the torch at them. Then descends the ramp with great care. Flashes the torch at SYLVIA)

LES: Hello, darling.

SYLVIA: Sod off!

LES: Charming.

(Flashes the torch on the jacket)

Are we all wearing each other's clothes now?

ANDY: She was cold.

LES: I'm bloody freezing.

(LES flashes the torch seawards)

What's the plan then?

(Pause)

See fuck all in this fog.

ANDY: Les . . .

LES: What?

ANDY: Sylvie's not well.

LES: No, she's pissed.

ANDY: Don't you think you ought to take her to bed?

44

LES: (drawls) What a topping idea!

    (LES formally offers his arm to SYLVIA)

SYLVIA: Fuck off!

LES: Now she's quoting me!

ANDY: Come on, Sylvie . . .

    (SYLVIA rises to join ANDY)

LES: Where are you going?

ANDY: I'll take her across to the hotel.

LES: You gonna put her to bed?

ANDY: I'll just take her across . . .

LES: I couldn't allow it.

ANDY: What?

LES: I couldn't let her go with you.

ANDY: Stop acting -

LES: Put my sweetheart in the clutches of a known
    lecher? I'd never forgive meself!

    (LES bars the way. ANDY lets go of SYLVIA. She
    sits down)

ANDY: Les . . .

LES: What, darling?

ANDY: She ought to be in bed.

LES: I second that.

ANDY: Let her go . . .

LES: She won't come with me.

    (LES flashes the torch at SYLVIA)

    She's gone off me . . .

ANDY: Lay off.

LES: (to SYLVIA) You gonna stay here all night?

SYLVIA: Yes!

LES: Won't do any good staying here. (then hearty) I
    know! Why don't we all go into town and get pissed?

SYLVIA: Huh!

LES: Did you speak?

45

SYLVIA: You're pissed already.

LES: You can talk.

SYLVIA: He can hardly stand up.

LES: (injured) I'm just . . . just getting my second wind.

(LES flashes the torch seaward and peers through the binoculars)

See fuck all here. Hardly see the water. It's like looking down the lavo.

(Silence)

Never find him in this fog.

ANDY: Sit down, Les.

LES: In this fog . . . you wouldn't find a liner, never mind a frigging dinghy. So what about it, mate?

ANDY: What?

LES: You're the brains of the operation.

ANDY: What do you mean?

LES: What's the plan?

ANDY: We wait.

LES: What? All night?

ANDY: Till he makes it.

LES: If he makes it. Coulda been rammed by a bloody liner, nobody'd ever notice.

(Silence)

Great night out, this. More like a bloody wake.

ANDY: I'll go up to the coastguards.

LES: Ahhhh . . . action!

SYLVIA: I'll come with you.

(ANDY walks up the ramp. SYLVIA follows. LES joins her - walks by her side. SYLVIA stops. LES stops. SYLVIA starts up the ramp and LES accompanies her. SYLVIA stops)

LES: Shall we dance?

SYLVIA: Are you going or not?

46

LES: I was just gonna ask you that.

(SYLVIA sits down)

You better give him his anorak back.

SYLVIA: What?

LES: Give him it back and you can have my jacket.

(LES starts taking off his jacket)

SYLVIA: (calls) Andy.

ANDY: (from the promenade) What?

SYLVIA: You better take your anorak.

ANDY: Don't worry about it.

LES: There's a gentleman for you.

(LES examines the bottle then offers it round. Silence. He drinks)

Nobody join me? You miserable bitches! Cheers!

Hey . . . did you hear about the man with red hair?

(pause) The body of a man with red hair was washed up on the Isle of Man.

JEAN: How did you hear that?

LES: Heard it on the radio.

JEAN: Well . . . Nick didn't have red hair.

SYLVIA: It was more of a light brown.

LES: It had golden glints in the sunlight.

(LES drains the bottle and throws it into the water)

JEAN: Did you mean that about the liner?

LES: What?

JEAN: Ramming the dinghy.

LES: Could happen.

JEAN: Anything could happen.

LES: It's a busy channel.

JEAN: But the chance of a collision . . .

LES: Wouldn't have to be a collision.

JEAN: What?

LES: Pass nearby would do it. Little boat like a dinghy,

47

get swamped in the wake of a powerboat. Wouldn't
have to touch. Nobody'd notice.

(LES goes to the side of the ramp)

'Scuse me, ladies . . . while I tap this kidney.

(He urinates)

SYLVIA: Don't listen to him . . .

JEAN: What?

SYLVIA: He's just trying to stir it up.

JEAN: Oh . . .

SYLVIA: I know . . . he's after blood.

JEAN: But what he said -

SYLVIA: He's exaggerating.

JEAN: Why?

SYLVIA: I told you - he's out for blood.

(LES comes back)

LES: Ladies shouldn't whisper.

JEAN: Were you exaggerating?

LES: Did she say that?

(LES flashes the torch in SYLVIA's face, then
JEAN's)

You believe me don't you?

SYLVIA: Leave her alone.

JEAN: Oh, let him play.

LES: Never had so many laughs in me life!

(LES stands at the front of the ramp and flashes the
torch out to sea: two short bursts, then one long,
then one short)

SYLVIA: What's he doing now?

LES: Distress signal.

SYLVIA: What?

LES: (shouts) "I AM DISABLED. COMMUNICATE WITH
ME."

JEAN: You'll have the coastguard in here next.

48

(LES focuses awkwardly on his watch)

LES: Jesus! Near eleven!

SYLVIA: Why don't you go to bed?

LES: (coy) If you come with me . . .

SYLVIA: Bugger off.

LES: Didn't come all the way to Dublin to sleep on me own.

(LES flashes the torch in a wide arc across the sea, slowly)

No sign. Nothing. Nobody there.

(Silence. ANDY comes down the ramp)

ANDY: I bumped into one of the coastguards. They've called off the search.

SYLVIA: Oh God . . .

ANDY: Till the fog lifts. They say it's even worse out there. It's hopeless searching . . . and it's danger-ous for the lifeboats.

JEAN: What about Nick?

ANDY: They've done all they can.

SYLVIA: What could have happened?

ANDY: If he had mechanical trouble then he's probably just riding it out.

JEAN: You mean drifting?

ANDY: I mean riding it out on the sea anchor. It's not a proper anchor . . . really only a kind of parachute you throw over the side and it fills with water and keeps you in place . . . holds you steady . . . well, pretty steady. (pause) They'll find him in the morning. (pause) They said they'd send a message across to the hotel if there's any . . . (pause) I suppose I better go and ring my missus . . .

JEAN: And his.

ANDY: What?

49

JEAN: Isn't his wife staying at your house tonight?

ANDY: Yeah, that's right.

JEAN: You'd better tell her the good news.

ANDY: Yeah . . . no point in them staying up all night
for nothing.

(ANDY starts up the ramp, stops)

Are you coming over?

JEAN: No.

ANDY: There's no point in staying here.

JEAN: Go and make your phone call.

ANDY: Sylvie . . .

SYLVIA: What?

ANDY: Don't you think you better get to bed?

LES: She wants to be here, in the reception committee.

(Silence)

(stands) I don't know about you but I came over to
see the inside of the pubs and that's what I'm gonna
do. How about you, Andy? (pause) We can keep in
touch with the hotel. Ring back every fifteen minutes.

ANDY: Yeah, we could.

LES: That's what Nick would do.

JEAN: If he'd had the radio . . .

LES: What?

JEAN: If only he'd the radio . . .

LES: He had a radio. I got him a radio.

JEAN: With flat batteries!

LES: He shoulda got new ones.

JEAN: You knew what would happen.

LES: I told him he was crazy.

JEAN: And then you got him the equipment . . .

LES: Christ, first I'm at fault for not getting the gear,
and now I'm at fault for getting it.

JEAN: He couldn't have gone otherwise.

50

LES: Anyway Nick was supposed to get his own equipment.
But I had to spend two whole days running round the
town getting it for him. He spent the whole of last
week in the alehouse talking about the trip - and
getting free drinks on the strength of it.

JEAN: I didn't see you refusing any.

LES: What?

JEAN: You were there with him. You encouraged him to
drink.

ANDY: Nick never needed much encouragement to drink.

JEAN: Oh, you were just as bad.

ANDY: Eh?

JEAN: Worse, in fact, because he trusted you. He thought
you were his friend.

ANDY: What are you on about?

JEAN: You encouraged him to spend all his time in the
pubs and in the clubs so he never got a stroke of work
done . . . wasting his life. I think you wanted to see
him go to pieces because you were jealous of him.
And that's why you encouraged him in this . . . this
madness . . .

SYLVIA: Jean, be fair!

JEAN: What?

SYLVIA: Everybody wanted to help Nick.

JEAN: Oh, you're all as bad, all of you.

SYLVIA: You can't blame them!

JEAN: It was you who encouraged him most of all.

SYLVIA: Me?

JEAN: You know . . .

SYLVIA: I didn't want him to sail.

JEAN: You know what I mean.

LES: What do you mean?

JEAN: (mocking) "Oh Nick you're so brave . . . "

SYLVIA: I never said that.

JEAN: I can imagine.

SYLVIA: You never heard me say that.

JEAN: What did you say?

(Pause)

LES: What are you saying?

JEAN: Don't you know?

(Silence)

SYLVIA: Christ . . . You're both writing him off.

LES: (to JEAN) What do you mean by saying she
encouraged Nick?

SYLVIA: You're both talking as if he had no chance.

LES: Shut up. (then to JEAN) What do you mean?

JEAN: Ask her.

LES: You seem to know a lot about it.

JEAN: I got it from the source.

LES: What are you talking about? (then to SYLVIA) What's
she talking about?

(SYLVIA jumps up to join ANDY)

SYLVIA: I don't know! I'm sick of both of you and your
squabbling -

(LES holds her)

LES: Tell me what she means.

SYLVIA: Leave me alone!

LES: When you tell me.

SYLVIA: Ask her. Ask her. I don't know.

LES: Don't you?

SYLVIA: NO!

LES: I think you do.

SYLVIA: Let me go. I feel sick!

(LES releases her and she slides to the ramp. He
stoops down by her)

LES: Sylvia . . . please . . .

52

SYLVIA: Leave me alone . . .

LES: I only wanted to know what she was -

(SYLVIA retches. LES turns and looks at JEAN)

Satisfied?

JEAN: What?

(LES slaps JEAN and she falls back. LES stands,
starts up the ramp)

LES: I'm going. I've had a bellyful of this -

JEAN: Nick had her in the back of the car last week on
the beach at Freshfield. Didn't you hear? It was all
round the alehouse.

(Silence. LES looks at JEAN. ANDY steps down the
ramp)

ANDY: Jean.

JEAN: Wasn't it?

LES: Is that true?

ANDY: For Christ's sake, Jean!

JEAN: Ask him.

LES: (to ANDY) Is that true?

(LES looks at ANDY. Silence. ANDY stoops to
SYLVIA. LES bars his way)

ANDY: She's sick . . .

LES: Hang on.

ANDY: Let's get her to bed.

LES: Is that true?

ANDY: All this fuss about a fuck . . .

(ANDY moves back from LES, LES stoops to
SYLVIA)

LES: I knew there was something. I could sense it. All
week I could sense something. And then I knew. When
he was sailing off I knew. You shouted: "Goodbye,
lover!" Didn't you? "Goodbye, lover!" That's what
you shouted to him. Those were your last words to

53

him. "Goodbye, lover!"

(LES touches SYLVIA's neck. She sobs)

Sylvia . . .

SYLVIA: What?

LES: (anguished) Why did you do it with him?

SYLVIA: I don't know what you want!

LES: What?

SYLVIA: I don't . . . (hysterical) I don't know what you
want of me. You say you want me and you make love
to me and you never . . . you never . . .

LES: What?

SYLVIA: . . . give . . .

LES: Give?

SYLVIA: You never give me anything . . .

LES: Oh Christ!

SYLVIA: You never give me any hope . . . for . . .

LES: (hard) Why did you let him do it?

(SYLVIA sobs. ANDY tries to get JEAN to go. She
doesn't move. ANDY stands uncertainly)

SYLVIA: And you turn on me and swear at me and . . .
mock me . . . and I don't . . . I don't know what you
want of me. I don't know!

(SYLVIA slumps down on the ramp. She retches.
LES stands)

ANDY: Let's get her to bed, Les.

LES: No.

ANDY: We've gotta get her to bed.

LES: You do it.

ANDY: What?

LES: One thing I could never do . . .

ANDY: What?

LES: Fuck a woman that's drunk.

(LES goes up the ramp)

ANDY: Les . . .

LES: What?

ANDY: You can't leave her . . .

LES: Can't I?

ANDY: She's sick.

LES: Is she? So am I.

ANDY: She needs you . . .

LES: I'd rather stick it in a jar of worms.

    (LES goes off)

ANDY: (stooping) Sylvie . . .

SYLVIA: I'm sorry . . .

ANDY: It's all right.

SYLVIA: Has he gone?

ANDY: Just lie still for a bit.

SYLVIA: (weeping) I didn't mean to . . . to . . .

ANDY: Shhhhh

SYLVIA: Jean . . .

    (JEAN looks at SYLVIA)

    I'm sorry . . . I was feeling so low . . .

ANDY: Don't worry about it.

SYLVIA: All I know is . . . I do love Les. I do. But he
    never gives me any hope! (sobbing) I know he won't
    forgive me but I do love him. He won't believe me
    but he's the one I love . . . the only one . . . He's
    the first man I ever loved and the only man I ever
    could love . . .

JEAN: Oh, belt up.

    (Silence. SYLVIA pulls herself up. She takes off
    ANDY's anorak and lets it fall to the ramp. She goes
    up to the top of the promenade and looks left and
    right)

SYLVIA: (shouts) Les. Les!

    (SYLVIA runs along the promenade and off. ANDY

steps up the ramp as if to follow then stops. Turns
and looks at JEAN. JEAN stares out to sea. Silence.
ANDY walks slowly up the ramp and off. JEAN sits
rigid, staring ahead. Yellow fog swirls around)
LIGHTS FADE
BLACKOUT

# ACT THREE

Scene: The next morning. A grey day with light rain.
JEAN sits on the ramp, huddled in a raincoat. ANDY
walks along the promenade, stops, looks out to sea
for a moment. Comes down the ramp. Glances at
JEAN, then looks through the binoculars.

ANDY: Thank God it's cleared up. (pause) Why don't you
go and get some breakfast? They're still serving.

JEAN: I don't want any.

ANDY: (hearty) What . . . when it's paid for?

JEAN: Mine isn't.

ANDY: What?

JEAN: I haven't got any money to pay the bill.

ANDY: Oh, don't worry about that. I'll look after that.
(Silence)
You ought to eat some breakfast. (pause) Seen any-
thing of Les and Sylvia?

JEAN: No.

ANDY: They weren't at breakfast. (pause) I always say
you should start the day with a good breakfast.
(Silence)
When did they start the search?

JEAN: First thing this morning, when the fog lifted.

ANDY: I didn't wake up till nine o'clock.

JEAN: Have you rung home?

ANDY: Eh? Oh, yes. Yes I spoke to the missus. You wouldn't believe it, but . . . she stayed up all night. I mean, she's never had a good word to say for Nick, but she stayed up all through the night.

JEAN: With his wife?

ANDY: Aye.

JEAN: Did you go into Dublin?

ANDY: I'd arranged to meet someone.

(Silence)

If I'd known you were gonna stay here all night . . .

JEAN: There wouldn't have been any point in you staying here.

ANDY: No, but . . .

JEAN: I'm sorry about last night.

ANDY: What?

JEAN: The things I said to you.

ANDY: Oh, forget it.

JEAN: I meant what I said to Les.

ANDY: It's best forgotten.

JEAN: No . . . I did mean it. (pause) Anyone can see he's got her on a string . . .

ANDY: He's a funny bloke.

JEAN: It just makes me mad to see the way he uses her. And she's so bloody naive . . .

ANDY: She's only in her teens.

JEAN: She'll be naive when she's ninety.

ANDY: She's innocent.

JEAN: She's not innocent, she's naive.

(Silence)

Nick and I had a terrible row about her.

ANDY: Did you?

JEAN: Seems so stupid now. But . . . he said she threw

58

herself at him. And I said if he had to jump into the
back of the car with every little cow that came along,
well . . . we might as well finish. (pause) It brought
things to a head, I didn't <u>want</u> to finish, but I thought
it might be better for him.

ANDY: Yeah . . .

JEAN: And he agreed . . .

ANDY: Did he?

JEAN: Then the next day he went down on his knees and
begged me to start again.

ANDY: Huh . . .

JEAN: I just blew up.

ANDY: Did you?

JEAN: I told him . . . said he didn't know what the hell
he wanted, or didn't want . . . me, or his wife, or
a string of little cows, or . . . or all of it or none of
it. And I asked him if he thought this . . . <u>this</u>
pantomime was going to solve anything.

ANDY: What did he say?

JEAN: He said, "No, but it'll be a laugh."

ANDY: Sounds like Nick.

JEAN: It was just . . . bravado. (pause) I didn't care if
he . . . screwed the odd scrubber now and again.
It meant nothing to me. I could stand it if he could.
But he couldn't . . . He let it go to his head.

ANDY: He's a romantic.

JEAN: What?

ANDY: I think what it was with Nick, he got married too
early. He was only in his teens when he married.
He never really had time to enjoy himself. And then
in his thirties he realised he'd missed out. He felt
cheated. But instead of being honest about it he
convinced himself there was some real change in

59

society. You know the way he used to rant on . . .
he looked at the teenagers and convinced himself
that they were free . . . sexually free, in a way we
hadn't been. Rubbish! We were all at it when we
were teenagers, just the same. Nothing's changed.
May be a bit more open nowadays, but that's all.
But Nick . . . he really swallowed all this rubbish
you read in the magazines . . .

JEAN: I think his trouble was that he still thought it was
an achievement if he slept with someone.

(LES comes down the ramp)

LES: No news . . .

ANDY: No. Thank God it's cleared -

LES: Bad.

ANDY: What?

LES: I would have thought they'd have spotted him by now.

ANDY: They've only had a couple of hours . . . give
them time . . .

(Silence. LES sits)

JEAN: There was a man at the coastguards' stayed up all
night trying to contact him on the radio . . . just in
case he could receive a message.

ANDY: Nick might have received it then.

JEAN: Hmmmmm.

ANDY: He's got all he needs to last for a week.

JEAN: Except the batteries.

LES: Don't start on that!

JEAN: That was the most important thing.

ANDY: Everything's important when you're out there.

LES: Look . . . look at this.

(LES takes a list from his pocket and tries to show
it to JEAN)

(reads) Spare jerrycan of petrol

First Aid box

Binoculars

Rope

Magnetic compass

Sea anchor

Torch

Alarm clock

Christ, he's got all he needs and more! Look, safety harness, food hamper, brandy, thermos flask -

JEAN: And you didn't put any sugar in the coffee.

LES: I what?

JEAN: You didn't put any sugar in his coffee.

LES: Christ!

JEAN: Nick can't drink coffee with no sugar in.

LES: Then he'll die of thirst.

JEAN: You can laugh.

LES: If he dies of thirst I'll never forgive myself.

(Silence)

If he'd allowed a bit more time for the preparations he could have had his sugar, and his batteries. But he was so bloody cocky - so eager to get away -

JEAN: Cocky?

LES: Yes, cocky . . . he talked as if he could wade across.

JEAN: He can't even swim.

LES: He can't swim?

JEAN: No.

LES: Jesus.

JEAN: He said it wouldn't make much difference anyway if . . .

LES: I suppose he might get a lift from a passing liner.

(Silence)

JEAN: Even at the last minute he might have called it off

if it hadn't been for you.

LES: Yeah, blame me.

JEAN: He said he wanted to call the trip off.

LES: When?

JEAN: When he was sitting in the dinghy . . .

LES: Oh yeah!

JEAN: I heard him say, "Let's call it off."

LES: He chickened out.

JEAN: He was worried about the engine.

LES: That was only an excuse.

JEAN: I heard him say it would never work.

LES: You think I was gonna let him get away with that after all I'd had to do? I fixed the sparking plugs, didn't I? And then he snapped the shearing pin on a rock when he was manoevring the dinghy to give the photographer a better shot. I had to go down into the water, dick first, to get to the propeller shaft. I got soaked to the waist while he was sitting there in his sailor cap chunnering away, "Let's have it, it'll never work!"

JEAN: And you pushed him off!

LES: Yes, I did. And I took great pleasure in doing it. I took three steps in the water and give the dinghy an almighty shove and shouted: "FUCK OFF TO IRELAND!"

(LES laughs sourly)

JEAN: I hope you're pleased now.

LES: Look . . . Nick would never have cancelled his trip with all the reporters there and all the pricks from the Yachting Club standing around laughing at him. He'd left it too late by then. You know that . . . he didn't want to be humiliated.

JEAN: I'd rather he'd been humiliated, than . . .

(Silence)

LES: You didn't help.

JEAN: What?

LES: The way you'd been carrying on.

JEAN: What do you mean?

LES: Ask Sylvia.

JEAN: About what?

LES: Sylvia and me, we had a talk last night.

JEAN: I'm surprised she could speak.

LES: She spoke enough to make me understand a bit more
    about Nick.

JEAN: What?

LES: She said that . . . that night . . . when they were
    out . . . he was in a pathetic state. Crying in his
    ale. (pause) He told her that he could have managed
    his job, and the drink would have been no problem,
    if it hadn't been for sex.

JEAN: What?

LES: He said sex was his only real problem, but it was
    fucking everything else up. If he wasn't getting hell
    from his wife, he was getting hell from you.

JEAN: That's not true.

LES: With you he'd looked for a second chance . . . but
    all he got was a second chain.

JEAN: That's not true!

LES: Isn't it?

JEAN: No.

LES: That's what Nick told Sylvia.

JEAN: If I chained him, it was because he wanted to be
    chained.

    (Silence)

    He did want to be . . .

    (LES laughs. JEAN stares at him, then goes off in

63

silence)

ANDY: I wonder where the bastard is.

LES: He mighta fucked off.

ANDY: Where?

LES: Anywhere.

ANDY: Anywhere?

LES: Africa.

ANDY: That's a long way.

LES: Further the better. Yeah . . . he might have shot
through to Africa. He always said he'd like to take
up white slave trading.

ANDY: I should've gone with him.

LES: What, slaving?

ANDY: No, trading.

    (Pause)

LES: He could have jumped a steamer, you know.

ANDY: You think so? (pause) Pardon me while I trump.
    (ANDY farts. Sits on the ramp, delicately)
Had a rough night last night.

LES: Oh aye?

ANDY: Boozing and whoring. Paid for it this morning,
though.

LES: How?

ANDY: The agony in the lavatory.

LES: (laughs) The squitters?

ANDY: What a way to start the day!

LES: What were you drinking?

ANDY: Home brewed stuff. Rotgut. (squirms) My arse
feels like a blood orange. I feel as though I'm sitting
on hot pips. Ohhh . . . I think I'll switch to pot in
future. (pause) Where's Sylvie?

LES: Having her breakfast.

ANDY: All right?

64

LES: All right.

ANDY: You know Jean stayed here all night?

LES: Did she?

ANDY: She's in a bad state.

LES: Playing the tragedy queen.

(ANDY looks through the binoculars)

ANDY: Yes, it's clearing up. (pause) I did something very strange this morning.

LES: What was that?

ANDY: Wiped my arse with my left hand.

LES: You musta been pissed.

ANDY: Very strange, that.

(LES looks through the binoculars)

LES: When you think of all the people that get involved in anything like this . . . like the coastguards, and the helicopter pilot, and the ships . . . and the bloke who stayed up on the radio . . . and us . . . and oh, everyone . . .

ANDY: People want to help.

LES: I'd charge anyone who was rescued with the cost of the rescue.

ANDY: Oh, you spoilsport!

(Silence)

LES: Why couldn't she wait in the hotel?

ANDY: I suppose she wanted to be here.

LES: To greet Nick as he came dripping outa the fog?

ANDY: I suppose so.

LES: She's as crazy as he is. Huh . . . I think we're all crazy.

ANDY: How did you get on last night?

LES: All right.

ANDY: How is Sylvia?

LES: All right.

ANDY: You can't afford to take these things too seriously, can you?

LES: Which?

ANDY: I mean . . . it's O. K. , having a bit on the side . . . everyone has a bit on the side, every man does, naturally . . . but you can't afford to let it upset you. I like a bit of strange as much as the next man, but I'd never let it interfere with the family. I think that was Nick's problem.

LES: What?

ANDY: I think you were right. Whatever Jean says, I think she wanted to get her hands on him for herself.

LES: Definitely.

ANDY: Nick said as much to me himself.

LES: Did he?

ANDY: She's been driving him up the wall of late. And you know where this . . . this expedition started?

LES: Where?

ANDY: Weeks ago . . . when we were planning the week-end. She suddenly announced she wanted to come on the weekend with us. Nick wouldn't hear of it.

LES: He didn't want her along?

ANDY: Never! But she kept bringing it up. She wasn't content to sit on the sidelines. She wanted to be with him all the time. I warned him it would happen. (pause) I'm sure she was even jealous of me! (pause) Then she said if he wouldn't take her he need not bother coming back.

LES: So he agreed . . .

ANDY: And then he came up with this idea.

LES: I see.

ANDY: I told him: Play around as much as you like, but don't let it spoil your family life. Don't let it affect

66

the wife and kids . . . they're the ones that really
count.

LES: How many kids have you got?

ANDY: Not enough.

LES: Eh?

ANDY: Never enough kids.

LES: How many?

ANDY: Four to date, but I'm working on the missus.

LES: You want more?

ANDY: Of course.

LES: And what about your missus?

ANDY: You know . . . people say a mother is closest to
her children, but I don't accept that. I believe that
a father is far closer. The times I have with those
kids! You should come with us one Sunday.

LES: Where?

ANDY: The park. Every Sunday morning - about this time
actually - I take them out to Mass, and then we go to
the park and fool around. Makes no difference if it's
raining or sunny, we enjoy ourselves. The oldest
kicks a ball around - when I look at him I can see
myself. I swear he'll make a centre forward for
Liverpool one day! And the little girl - she's only
that high - she comes up to me and says:"Daddy, I
can't find any fairies in the grass!" And I help her
to search for fairies in the grass! (laughing) Makes
me feel young again. Yes, really . . . when I play
with my kids, I say I'm doing it for their sake, but
I'm not . . . I'm doing it for myself. I mean . . .
it's keeping me young!

LES: Does your wife go with you?

ANDY: Their mother doesn't play with them like that.
(pause) Marriage changes a woman more than it does

67

a man. Mind you . . . they get on all right with
her . . .

LES: How do you get on with her?

ANDY: Oh, she's a good woman. Good mother. I wouldn't
hear a word said against her. (pause) But she's not
the woman I love . . .

LES: Isn't she?

ANDY: No.

LES: Who's that?

ANDY: Oh, no one you would know. A woman I knew
years ago in my teens. We had a marvellous
relationship . . . madly in love, both of us . . .
but it just wasn't the right time for us. (pause) She
got married and had a family . . . and I got married
and had my family . . .

LES: Do you ever see her?

ANDY: I haven't seen her in ages. But after all these
years and after hundreds of other women, I know
that she was the one . . . of all of them, she was
the one I really loved. I still do.

LES: Did you see Fat Annie?

ANDY: What?

LES: Last night . . . did you see Fat Annie?

ANDY: Oh, Annie . . . yeah . . . yeah, I saw her. I was
standing in the pub, looking at the door, a plate
glass door. And suddenly the glass went dark and a
great shape blocked out the light.

LES: Fat Annie?

ANDY: Fatter Annie.

LES: Fatter?

ANDY: Yeah . . . fatter. Jesus, she was the one woman
I would have sworn could never put on weight, she
was that fat already.

68

LES: Does it turn you on?

ANDY: What?

LES: Her being that fat?

ANDY: No . . . (laughs) No, not really.

LES: But you fucked her?

ANDY: Yes.

LES: Did you fancy her?

ANDY: I didn't fancy her but I just couldn't resist the
    obscenity of it.

LES: Kinky.

ANDY: We lay in front of a roaring fire and I dined off
    roast arse.

LES: Tasty?

ANDY: My favourite dish . . . I'd eat it but for the hairs.
    (They laugh)

LES: I should've come with you.

ANDY: Did you have a good night?

LES: Hilarious.

ANDY: (laughing) What did you do?

LES: Sylvia threw up in the bedroom so I cleaned it all up
    and put her to bed, and sat and drank a bottle of
    Scotch while she slept.

ANDY: I thought you were gonna have some wild sex.

LES: After last night?

ANDY: A reconciliation followed by a good fuck . . .
    nothing like it!

LES: Anyway she was unwell.

ANDY: What?

LES: She had the rags up.

ANDY: The best time of all!

LES: Eh?

ANDY: Women are always at their randiest during a
    period.

LES: Ugggh . . .

ANDY: What?

LES: All that blood!

ANDY: Shhh . . .

   (SYLVIA comes on, walks down the ramp)

   Well . . . what have you got to say for yourself?

SYLVIA: What?

ANDY: (mock stern) Don't come the little innocent with
   me Miss. What about last night?

SYLVIA: What happened?

ANDY: Don't you know?

SYLVIA: My mind just blanked out.

ANDY: Just as well.

SYLVIA: What did I do?

ANDY: I'll spare you the memory.

   (SYLVIA sits. ANDY looks through the binoculars)

   The ferry's coming in.

SYLVIA: When does it leave?

ANDY: About an hour or so.

SYLVIA: We'll have to catch it.

ANDY: You got to go back?

SYLVIA: Are you going to stay?

ANDY: I don't know. I think I'll go and talk to the coastguards . . .

SYLVIA: If I wasn't back tonight my mother would have
   the police out after me. Anyway, I'll have to be back
   for work tomorrow.

ANDY: There's no call for that sort of language.

SYLVIA: What?

ANDY: "Work"!

SYLVIA: I'm sorry. (pause) What are we going to do?

ANDY: What?

SYLVIA: About Nick?

70

ANDY: Order a wreath.

SYLVIA: Oh, Andy!

ANDY: I've been trying to decide between lilies and carnations.

SYLVIA: You're completely heartless.

ANDY: No disrespect.

SYLVIA: Huh . . .

ANDY: I mean, it comes to us all. You know, it's at times like this you really appreciate the value of your religion. It's funny . . . only last week I was in that little church near the Pier Head. Yes, I was passing, and I went in and knelt down for a bit. The alehouse was open and by rights I should have been in there. But I just had this impulse and I went in, and came out feeling strengthened.

SYLVIA: And then you went into the alehouse.

ANDY: Yes, and felt fortified.

SYLVIA: Nick wasn't religious, though, was he?

ANDY: Oh aye.

SYLVIA: He never talked about it.

ANDY: Oh, he had many failings but he still had his faith.

LES: We'll have to compose a message of condolence.

ANDY: We'll pick one out of the newspaper.

LES: "Never forgotten, always rotten."

(Silence)

ANDY: What if he turned up?

LES: Last we'll see of him.

SYLVIA: What?

LES: He's well away.

ANDY: Suppose he turned up and we'd all gone home?

LES: He could turn round and sail back.

SYLVIA: It would be awful, though, if he did turn up . . .

LES: Does it bother you?

71

SYLVIA: No, but . . .

LES: You wanna stay here?

SYLVIA: No. No.

(Silence. ANDY stands)

ANDY: If we're gonna catch the ferry I'd better go and
talk to Jean.

LES: She'll probably want to stay here.

ANDY: But we've all got responsibilities . . . I mean,
we've got to get back, haven't we?

LES: She's got responsibilities too.

ANDY: We can't wait here indefinitely.

SYLVIA: She looks exhausted.

ANDY: She was stupid staying up all night.

(Silence)

SYLVIA: I can't help feeling sorry for her.

LES: She'll take it out on her husband.

ANDY: You know . . . a thing like this makes you think.
It reminds you of basic values. Take Nick. I mean,
there he was . . . with a good wife, lovely kids, a
good job. And he threw it all away. Why? He was
always carrying on about being free. "Free" . . .
what the hell is that? He forgot the basic values . . .
lost touch with his roots. Went haywire. I mean, you
can take a drink without being an alcoholic. And you
can have sex without being a sex maniac. But Nick . . .
Nick really swallowed all this rubbish about permiss-
iveness. Huh! Permission to what? Permission to
ruin your life? Because that's what he did. (pause)
Anyway, people are fed up with it now. It's not
human, it's not real, it's just a fad. The pendulum
is swinging back. It's already happened in America!
(Silence. LES and SYLVIA look up at ANDY. ANDY
stands still for a moment, then goes up the ramp

and off. SYLVIA looks out to sea)

LES: (wry) "The pendulum is swinging back."

    (Pause)

    You shoulda heard his sermon on the joys of father-
hood.

SYLVIA: He's always going on about his children.

LES: I wonder if there'll be any more fathers like him . . .
in the future.

SYLVIA: He's very fond of his kids.

LES: He's a dying breed . . . poor bastard.

SYLVIA: What?

LES: When they grow up he'll be shattered.

SYLVIA: And what about you?

LES: What?

SYLVIA: When yours grow up . . . ?

LES: I was shattered when they were born.

SYLVIA: Didn't you want a family?

LES: I never thought about it.

SYLVIA: But you did want them . . . at the time?

LES: I did and I didn't. (pause) I never thought much
about it at the time.

SYLVIA: Did you discuss it with your wife?

LES: We just had them. (pause) Oh, I know it sounds
crazy but . . . but everyone else had kids, it seemed
to be the natural thing to do. It was only after they
arrived I realised I didn't want them.

SYLVIA: How do you get on with them?

LES: All right.

SYLVIA: Do you?

LES: Yeah, I get on all right with them. I'm a model bad
father, but I get on with them all right.

    (Pause)

SYLVIA: Don't you like children?

LES: It's not that.

SYLVIA: What then?

LES: I don't want to look after them.

SYLVIA: That's the woman's job.

LES: I don't want her to look after them then.

SYLVIA: It's natural for a woman to want children.

LES: What about Jean?

SYLVIA: What?

LES: She doesn't want children.

SYLVIA: She only says that because of Nick.

LES: Seems like everyone who wants them hasn't got them and everyone who's got them doesn't want them.

(Silence)

SYLVIA: Les . . .

LES: What?

SYLVIA: About last night . . .

LES: Oh, skip it.

SYLVIA: I'm sorry.

LES: Doesn't matter.

SYLVIA: I want it to matter. (pause) I think I'm beginning to understand you a bit better now.

LES: What is there to understand?

SYLVIA: You won't flare up?

LES: Do you wanna go back to the hotel?

SYLVIA: I want to talk.

(Silence)

What happened with Nick didn't matter. It didn't matter to me.

LES: Didn't it?

SYLVIA: No.

LES: That's all right, then.

SYLVIA: You're still mad.

LES: I'm not mad.

74

SYLVIA: You are . . . aren't you?

(Silence)

LES: The best relationship I ever had with a woman was with a prostitute I met in Hamburg. I couldn't speak a word of German, and she couldn't speak any English. I stayed with her every night for a fortnight. Sixty marks a night was the going rate. And in the morning she used to give me hot brutwurst with bags of mustard.

SYLVIA: Brutwurst?

LES: Sausages.

SYLVIA: Oh . . .

LES: The last morning she cried.

SYLVIA: She cried?

LES: Yes . . . I think I cried a bit too. But five minutes later my tears dried up, and I knew hers had too. (pause) That was the best relationship I ever had with a woman.

(Silence)

SYLVIA: Don't be bitter.

LES: You think that's bitter? (laughs) It's a treasured memory, sweetheart. (pause) Nick's out of it all, now. In a way I almost admire him.

(Silence)

Why do you think Nick took the dinghy?

SYLVIA: He liked sailing.

LES: Huh!

SYLVIA: He did!

LES: You know Andy wanted to sail with him?

SYLVIA: No.

LES: He did.

SYLVIA: I'd never have expected Andy -

LES: He was dead keen, but Nick insisted on sailing solo.

SYLVIA: Nick lives in a dream world.

LES: So does Andy.

SYLVIA: He doesn't strike me like that.

LES: All that crap he comes out with!

SYLVIA: What?

LES: He's dead.

SYLVIA: Dead?

LES: He goes to church and his faith is dead. He has
women, and the sex is dead. He worships his family,
and that's dead. You know he and his wife are always
at each other's throats? I saw her one Saturday
morning at the supermarket and she had a black eye
and a mouthful of blood.

SYLVIA: I'd never have thought of Andy as violent.

LES: The only difference between Andy and Nick was
that Nick didn't fool himself. He fooled almost
everyone else but I don't think he fooled himself.
(Silence)

SYLVIA: I think all of you got married too young.

LES: You mean we should have waited?

SYLVIA: Yes.

LES: At least it would have shortened the agony.
(LES laughs)

SYLVIA: Do you think we would end up like that?

LES: Like what?

SYLVIA: Like Andy . . . or Nick . . .

LES: Or me?

SYLVIA: You're different. (pause) You are different.

LES: I'm no different.
(Silence)

SYLVIA: Have you ever had a fight with your wife?

LES: Yeah.

SYLVIA: A physical fight?

76

LES: Yes. That's what puts me off . . .

SYLVIA: What?

LES: You and me.

SYLVIA: We wouldn't . . . we wouldn't have to get married.

LES: It's not marriage.

SYLVIA: What is it then?

LES: I don't know. (pause) Can you understand me when I say that, if my mates had told me some fantastically sexy bird had fallen madly in love with me and was dying to meet me . . . then I would have run a mile?

SYLVIA: Oh aye . . .

LES: I would.

SYLVIA: Why?

LES: That's not what I want.

SYLVIA: What do you want?

LES: I don't want that.

(Silence)

SYLVIA: Did you ever fancy going with Nick?

LES: Sailing?

SYLVIA: Yes.

LES: No chance!

SYLVIA: But you knew more about sailing than any of them.

LES: I gave up sailing when I left the Navy.

SYLVIA: Do you ever think of going back in?

LES: I've had all that.

(Pause)

SYLVIA: I am sorry about . . . about Nick, and . . .

LES: It was bound to happen.

SYLVIA: It wasn't!

LES: If it hadn't been you it would have been me.

(Pause)

SYLVIA: Les . . .

LES: What?

SYLVIA: I would like to go on seeing you.

LES: So would I.

SYLVIA: But . . . is there any point?

LES: What?

SYLVIA: What is there to look forward to?

LES: Now?

SYLVIA: Yes.

LES: Nothing.

SYLVIA: Nothing?

LES: Nothing except seeing each other.

SYLVIA: I don't think that's enough.

LES: What do you want? A guarantee?

SYLVIA: No.

LES: I mean, how can I say . . . how do I know . . . Oh, Christ.

(Silence)

SYLVIA: There isn't anyone else, is there?

LES: Only my wife.

SYLVIA: I don't mean that.

LES: No.

SYLVIA: D'you think we ought to finish?

LES: All right.

SYLVIA: You want us to finish?

LES: As long as I can see you tomorrow.

SYLVIA: What?

LES: I could stand the thought of not sharing a life with you but I couldn't stand not seeing you tomorrow.

SYLVIA: Oh, Les.

(SYLVIA sobs, kisses LES. JEAN comes on)

JEAN: It's all right!

78

SYLVIA: What?

JEAN: They're coming in now!

LES: What?

(JEAN seizes the binoculars. Peers out to sea, then
runs up the ramp and looks from the promenade)

SYLVIA: Oh thank God . . .

LES: Who told you?

JEAN: A porter at the hotel. The coastguards have sent
a motor launch out.

(LES joins JEAN)

LES: Can I have a look?

(JEAN gives him the binoculars and he looks)
There's something there . . .

JEAN: Let me see!

(LES returns the binoculars)

LES: It's only a speck . . .

JEAN: Where? I can't see . . .

(LES points. JEAN stands on the railing)

LES: Over there . . . could be anything.

JEAN: I see it. I see it!

LES: What is it?

JEAN: It's a small boat.

LES: Can I have a look?

(LES peers through the binoculars. SYLVIA rushes
up the ramp and hugs JEAN)

SYLVIA: When did you hear?

JEAN: Now. Only just now!

LES: It's the launch. Towing the dinghy in.

JEAN: Oh, let me see!

(JEAN looks)

LES: See it?

JEAN: I see the launch . . . and oh God, yes, there's
the dinghy.

79

(ANDY comes along the promenade to the ramp.
JEAN sees him, hugs him. She looks out to sea
again through the binoculars)

SYLVIA: Can I see?

(SYLVIA looks through the binoculars)
Oh, there they are!

(SYLVIA hugs JEAN, both sobbing and laughing)

JEAN: Oh thank God . . . I'd never have forgiven myself
if . . . if . . . All last night I sat there and all I
could think was "He's gone." All I could say to
myself over and over again was "He's gone . . . he's
gone." And I . . . and I thought of the last time we
were together . . . a row. We had a stupid row . . .
I was crazy with jealousy, I couldn't stop myself . . .
I saw how selfish I'd been . . . when he was crying
out for help all I could see were my own miseries.
(sobs) With all the problems he had, I wasn't helping
him. I knew he needed me but instead of helping him
I was destroying him . . .

(As she speaks ANDY joins LES)

ANDY: She doesn't know.

LES: What?

ANDY: The boat was empty.

LES: Empty?

ANDY: Riding on the sea anchor.

LES: Oh Christ . . .

ANDY: All they're bringing in is the boat.

(LES looks up at JEAN in silence)

LES: You better tell her.

(JEAN stands high on the ramp)

JEAN: I was so selfish I couldn't see how desperate he
was himself. I couldn't help him. But now I know . .
yes, now I know . . .

BLACKOUT